EFFECTIVE LEADERSHIP

Tips to motivate and inspire your team members

Written by Bertrand de Witte

Translated by Carly Probert

Coaching 50MINUTES.com

EFFECTIVE LEADERSHIP   1

INSPIRING LEADERSHIP: THE BASICS   4

Leadership in enterprise

Are you a leader in the making?

Types of leadership

TOP TIPS   19

FAQS   21

What are the 12 essential qualities of a good leader?

Can a manager become a leader?

Can a leader become a manager?

How can I gain the trust of my team?

How can I restore my leadership if power games have disrupted my team?

Is it manipulative to exercise leadership?

What should a leader do in an organisation where leadership is not valued?

OVER TO YOU   26

FURTHER READING   30

EFFECTIVE LEADERSHIP

- **Problem:** How can I become a great leader?
- **Uses:** Being a good leader allows you to fully participate in the management of people and thus strengthen the motivation of employees and achieve your top objectives.
- **Professional uses:** Team management, business management.
- **FAQs:**
  - What are the 12 essential qualities of a good leader?
  - Can a manager become a leader?
  - Can a leader become a manager?
  - How can I gain the trust of my team?
  - How can I restore my leadership if power games have disrupted my team?
  - Is it manipulative to exercise leadership?
  - What should a leader do in an organisation where leadership is not valued?

Leadership is demonstrated in four main areas: private companies, businesses, politics and the military. In this book, we will focus on leadership in business.

Assessing the effectiveness of leadership in the professional world depends heavily on the culture of the company. As a quality that is increasingly valued, leadership is now part of job descriptions, discussed in annual assessments and features in training programs. Companies are likely to develop leadership within their management team, and ambitious employees often seek to exert their own influence.

Leadership is a true asset to team leaders or those who want to become a manager.

> "I'm not there to see what my teams report, or if they are working properly. I am here to make sure that the employees understand their mission, have the means necessary to succeed, cooperation is going well, and they are able to develop their talents. We do two annual surveys to find out if those responsible are managers and if employees feel inspired and motivated." – *Thierry Geerts – Country Manager, Google Belgium-Luxembourg*

To avoid mistakes that could compromise your career, this book offers numerous tips, illustrated by testimonies from experts and various business decision makers. Armed with these tools, you will improve your business skills. In addition, your strengthened leadership skills will allow you to follow a healthy and progressive career. They will make you a confident leader who is appreciated by your (future) team.

To do this, we will focus on the essential concepts needed for understanding leadership as seen in business today. You will discover how leadership is a competitive advantage, and learn to identify the difference between management and leadership. We will then turn to identify what makes a good leader and what skills they have. Finally, we will look at the different types of leaders and the different styles of leadership and team management.

The rest of this book is devoted to the practice of these elements, through advice, questions and answers, and finally, the application of a method to boost your career, evolving from an operational manager to a leader.

INSPIRING LEADERSHIP: THE BASICS

Leadership and management

Often confused, some clarification between the roles of a leader and a manager is necessary. The distinction between management and leadership was established, among others, by Abraham Zaleznik (1976) and John P. Kotter (1999). What do these two authors state?

- Management is the use of authority to manage resources and constraints in order to produce goods or services. The manager will therefore use their formal authority, authority given to them by their superiors and confirmed in their job description: their superiors have entrusted them to perform certain tasks. The manager manages, organises and controls complexity. They translate problems into solutions. They plan and manage their team according to short and medium-term logic. They have a functional role in the operation. When considering how to proceed, a manager usually starts by asking "How?".
- On the other hand, leadership is the ability to exert influence to achieve goals. A leader is able to inspire their employees to adhere to an idea or a project, mobilising them to achieve set objectives. They have a long-term outlook that they share and around which they construct their team. A leader seeks answers to questions that often begin with "Why?".

Manager or leader?

MANAGER	LEADER
Formal • Appointed by hierarchy and imposed on the team • Has formal authority • Is "above" • Receives an official title	**Informal** • Recognised as a leader by the team • Has influential and charismatic authority • Acts "alongside" • Takes a function, plays a role
Manager • Structures • Organises • Drives • Makes operational • Stays rational • Controls • Plans processes • Gives ideas	**Visionary** • Orients • Has a strategy • Guides and coaches • Creates change and momentum • Encourages innovation • Delegates • Seeks surprising results • Creates an environment that values the ideas of everyone
Goodwill • Focuses on tasks • Develops actions • Uses the team • Inspires fear • Supervises and gives permission	**Influence** • Focuses on people • Develops talents • Gives credit to the team • Generates enthusiasm • Supports and shares
Commands • Says "I..." • Says "You are going to..."	**Asks** • Says "We..." • Says "We are going to..."

Providing leadership therefore corresponds to a more emotional approach than management. A leader motivates their employees by creating a sense of belonging and showing gratitude. They also manage change with skill when dealing with uncertainties. Their actions become shining examples and inspire employees to believe in them and in themselves. A leader translates things by finding meaning and coherence. They make you want to follow them because they inspire trust.

Nevertheless, the distinction between a manager and a leader is rather tenuous. Great leaders naturally overlap their managerial skills and their leadership qualities. They cannot isolate one from the other.

> "Instead of the term 'leadership', I prefer something like 'director' that connects the concepts related to influence, relationships, listening, authority, confidence, creativity, the alignment of actions and words, the meaning of a team, action, decision and reflection.
> Therefore, distinguishing between the words 'leader' and 'manager' seems pointless to me. As a warship commander engaged for weeks in international crisis areas, I learned to lead, or in other words, to control in the heat of the moment, when time leaves no room for dialogue, and to manage in the interval time for the preparation and development of the solidarity of the army. It is primarily the context of space-time that must ultimately guide a potential leader in his action." – *Admiral Olivier Lajous, Former HRD in the French Navy*

Leadership and corporate culture

A person with great leadership skills will flourish more

in a corporate environment that leaves a wide space for creativity.

Leadership can indeed hardly be exercised in a highly Taylorised organisation, where work is divided, tasks are simple and repetitive, and employees are supervised by a manager of coercive power within a very directive system. Decision-making power is centralised at the top of the hierarchy, leaving little room for initiative. Although line work symbolises this type of business, there are many leaders who still operate Taylorism in their professional practices, both in the industrial and commercial sectors of administration.

Conversely, start-ups and companies that are known as flexible or liberal (Getz, 2012) evolve by being aware of instability and quickly find innovative responses. In this type of model, corporate culture values initiative and innovation. Leadership is collaborative and is shared in true independent teams with the values and purpose of the organisation.

Of course, these two models are complete opposites, and there are a vast majority of organisations where leadership is expressed in a diversified manner. A leader has an interest in finding a place where creativity and latitude are equally offered.

Leadership: a competitive advantage

Do you already possess technical and/or managerial skills? To go further, you will also need leadership qualities.

In a changing world, where adaptation and innovation mean a competitive advantage – or survival -, companies are in search of personalities who are able to produce and drive strategic change more than ever. Today, globalisation and new technologies require us all to rethink our business models in one way or another. Change becomes inevitable and its frequency increases regularly. To stay competitive, management alone is not enough. At large, organisations need men and women who are wise and creative, able to cope with uncertainties, mobilise resources and create meaning in a phase of organisational transformation and/ or adverse conditions.

LEADERSHIP AT NESTLÉ

Born out of innovation in 1866, and by dint of constant adaptations, Nestlé became the top company world-wide in the agribusiness sector, which was a particu-larly unstable environment. In 1997, Nestlé published its *"Principles of Management and Leadership"*, a tangible expression of the corporate culture that must be applied by all employees. The publication outlines the values, leadership assessment criteria, principles and commitments of the management group in leadership. In short, the criteria are: personal commit-ment, initiative, encouragement, motivation, curiosity, innovation, adaptation and intercultural skills. Thus, the selection of internal candidates for positions of high responsibility would depend on the application of these criteria, but also on their professional skills, their experience and their determination to get results.

Continuing education allows everyone to progress and flourish based on their area of expertise and personal skills. Nestlé encourages staff at all levels to contribute to the development of the company by providing "improvements that will promote both business results and personal development".

ARE YOU A LEADER IN THE MAKING?

A true leader can be identified by four components: their role in a group, their vision, their aura and their skills and talents.

Role in a group

As a leader, you naturally take the lead, i.e. you drive the group. You are able to lead the team, while introducing innovation. Similarly, you can manage to both deconstruct the established and usual elements and reconstruct new ideas by making them as legitimate as possible. The goal here is to involve the group in a process of change by leading them. You lead the passing from a comfort zone (sometimes already established) to a new, necessary zone. You lead the team through the forest, taking them from branch to branch. If there is a fall, you encourage, until everyone is convinced that they must continue the process.

Vision

You show leadership when there is a crisis, a major goal or something you want to exceed. The leadership challenge develops in a context. You have identified the issues that concern you and the situation is stronger than you, making you feel compelled to get involved. Gandhi, Martin Luther King and Nelson Mandela were all world leaders because they led a long non-violent struggle against injustice and racism.

Aura

Your charisma is known in the organisation. Ask yourself about your popularity: what are your actions or distinctive elements that have contributed to your reputation? Each moment and each of your characteristics will enhance your leadership. You are surprising both in your performance and in your habits. Some famous examples: the successive battles of Napoleon, the famous "I have understood you" speech by Charles de Gaulle, and the emblematic cigars of Churchill and Fidel Castro. We can recall a story, a success or a trademark of a great world leader and a leader that we encounter in the world of work because their aura is so impressive.

Skills and talents

Your success is inextricably linked to the demonstration of your ability. You are recognised as being gifted, as a competent person, whatever the area in which this ability is expressed. You also have a knack for surrounding yourself with people who have complementary skills. Your expertise inspires those around you and ensures high credibility. Today we can include the great innovators of new technologies: Steve Jobs (Apple), Larry Page (Google), as well as Richard

Branson (Virgin Group), Ingvar Kamprad (Ikea), Taiichi Ohno (Toyota Production System), etc.

A leader must combine professional and personal skills (Kouzes and Posner, 2012).

- Professional skills
    - The leader shows the way, i.e. they clearly explain the purpose of the journey: there is an aspiration and values to defend.
    - They inspire a shared vision. They express their great aspirations and respond to the question "What do we want to become?".
    - A leader tries to explain this situation and puts things forward in a structured way, in order to identify opportunities to seize. They develop a tactic.
    - They develop the conditions for success. They encourage. They are always positive, and they are the coach who advises and inspires confidence.
    - A leader is also not afraid to get their hands dirty, especially during difficult times. They explain that all tasks are vital to reach to target and participate to encourage everyone. This exemplary behaviour distinguishes them from others.

- Personal skills
    - A leader possesses power over others and on

the organisation, where they are one of the main players in terms of innovation or staff management.

- ○ They are genuine, because they believe in what they do. A leader who is not loyal to their values is quickly unmasked and discredited.
- ○ They are legitimate because they have experience.
- ○ Through their charisma, they understand, gather, motivate and influence people. They display brilliant emotional intelligence.

The eight leader archetypes (Kets de Vries, 2008)

According to Kets de Vries, leadership development can take one of eight directions. This typology allows you to identify your leadership style and note your strengths and weaknesses. These different orientations are cumulative, but through situations during your journey, some will be more dominant and others less prominent. You can strengthen your leadership by working on your weaknesses.

- **The builder:** You are the architect of a major project or large-scale plan. A great visionary, your ambitions can change the world (no matter how small) by exceeding the expectations of your contemporaries. Your vision, often humanist, relies on values.
- **The transactor:** your goal is to create harmony around you, bringing people together by weaving a link between

them and you. You make group members work together on a project or projects; unlike the builder leader, you do not work primarily for a single purpose.

- **The communicator:** without necessarily being a rhetorical whizz, you speak and touch people. You are comfortable speaking in public and defending your ideas.
- **The strategist:** you are a strategist when you manage to construct different methods and adapt them to each situation, reaching your goals despite actions to disrupt your plans. You are able to influence and bring back situations to your advantage.
- **The change-catalyst:** you demonstrate leadership when it suits you; for you, leadership is more of a capability to inspire additional development, performance and power.
- **The innovator:** you have to create, it is in your nature. You explore, discover, test and improve. You master the technical things. You are full of creativity and dream of being recognised as a pioneer.
- **The processor:** your operational management skills complement your ability to use your creativity and emotional intelligence.
- **The coach:** you believe in individual capacity and look to develop people's potential.

Oriented leadership (Blake and Mouton, 1987)

Some people feel more comfortable driving teams; others are more oriented towards production. From these general guidelines, it is possible to identify five major types of management, involving different leadership styles.

Oriented leadership

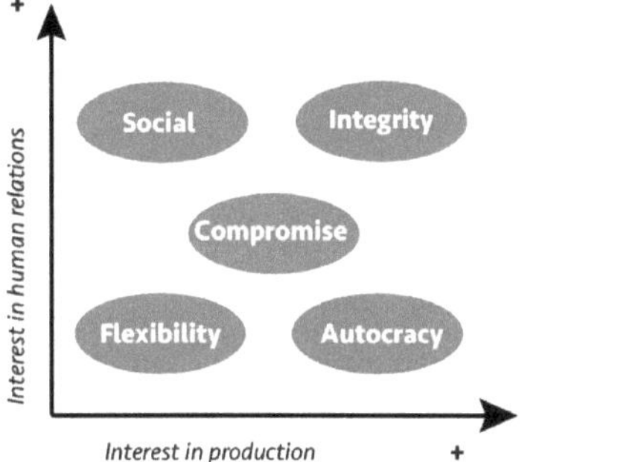

- **Authoritarian:** your interest is high for production and low for human relations. You plan, manage and direct, focusing mainly on processes and goals. You demand obedience and punish if rules are not respected.
- **Impoverished:** your interest in production and human relations is low, and you leave the team members to make their own decisions, concerning yourself only with the results. A believer in self-regulation, you think the group will come up with their own solutions. This prevents you from taking responsibility and allows you to pull profits without committing. Your management style almost goes against leadership: you are a sort of anti-leader.
- **Country club:** you give priority to good relationships within the group. You do not worry too much about production. You do not like taking control and prefer to please others by meeting their needs.
- **Middle of the road:** (between production and human relations): you negotiate to reach easy goals and maintain

a healthier social climate by favouring motivation rather than giving orders.

- **Team:** your interest in production is as high as your interest in social relations. You are a complete leader since, by fostering a climate of trust, you elicit the genuine commitment of your team to achieve set objectives. You encourage your team and involve them in decision-making, both operationally and in process control.

> "At ING Belgium the important thing is not only the achievement of business results. All employees and all managers are evaluated on how they achieve those results, i.e. their ability to be responsible and independent, collaborate and help their colleagues and to continually improve on customer service.
>
> To inspire their employees to want to live out the corporate culture, the role of our leaders is crucial. They are one of the first vehicles in this positive momentum, as their exemplary behaviour motivates employees.
>
> I come across many different styles of leaders in the organisation. For me, an essential quality is their dedication to the development of the company, and not to achieve their personal ambitions, the confidence and independence they offer to their employees, and their ability to concretely assist and support their teams in case of difficulties." – *Catherine Dedobbeleer – HR Project Manager, Organisational Effectiveness, ING Belgium*

Leading a team towards autonomy

Your group's performance level largely depends on your leadership style. The situational leadership theory (Paul Hersey and Kenneth H. Blanchard, 1977) will help you to make the right decisions, based on contextual variables. Your leadership style must be adapted to the maturity level of the person or group, so that everyone can gain autonomy. Therefore, there are stages in group maturity and leadership.

Situational leadership

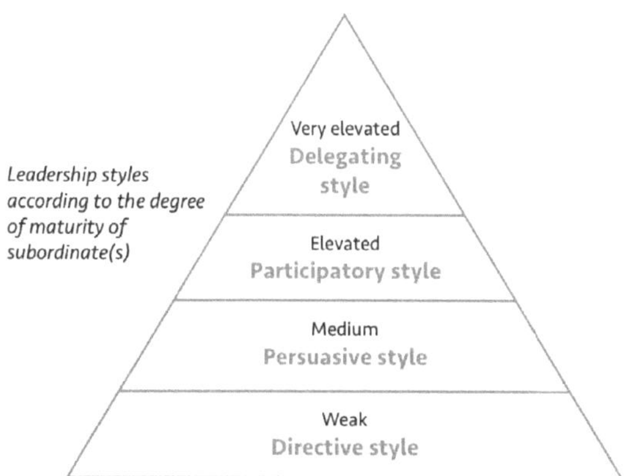

- **Telling.** The first level. You lead by explaining what to do and how to do it. You provide resources and feedback. You talk in terms of organisation, instruction and supervision.
- **Selling.** Trust and communication are better than the previous level. You train and convince your team by mobilising information and arguments. Your stories guide the team towards a goal. You are focused on demonstration, conviction and mobilisation. Remember, evidence is the greatest tool for convincing.

- **Participating.** Once your team is formed and ready to mobilise, you participate in the actions and decisions yourself. This step allows you to focus more on the relationship, rather than the direction and control. You work with the team and negotiate on sharing your decision-making responsibilities. You enter a phase where you give your team the ability to work independently. You are focused on listening, consulting and negotiating.
- **Delegating.** You continue the transfer of responsibilities. Mutual trust leads to positive experiences. You empower your team and give it leeway to operate on its own initiative. You keep an eye on what you have conveyed and allow the team to take risks. To remain the leader, your team should not be fully involved in (major) decisions. The regular help you provide is really appreciated by the team members. In case of difficulty, do not break trust and remember that you also have a responsibility.

> "Since its inception, I have contributed to the expansion of EXKI, first in Brussels and then in Paris, and now in New York. For each location, my role was to quickly create an effective team.
>
> In my career, I have learned that driving a team towards autonomy means encouraging the accountability of each member, starting with the team leader. They should be given all the necessary support and gradually lead them towards becoming self-reliant. Also, all employees must understand their mission and be encouraged. It is sometimes difficult to direct everything at once, but when the team is structured, responsible, and everyone takes part in its success, I can then go back to opening new markets.
>
> Autonomy is an area of realisation and expression, which

Leadership is developed through experience. Leadership is not innate, it is learned. A manager wishing to move their career forward needs to develop their leadership skills.

TOP TIPS

- Work on your **emotional intelligence**: get to know yourself to better measure your efforts and express your wishes; be fully aware of others, understand them and maintain relationships with them; control and suppress your impulses and moods that disturb rationality (i.e. do not manipulate and do not enforce discipline when angry).

EMOTIONAL INTELLIGENCE

Emotional intelligence is the ability to perceive your emotions and those of others, to be aware of them, understand them, and let them express themselves. It then becomes possible to regulate your own emotions and those of others in a group. This ability is an undeniable asset in business.

- Have a clear **vision**: look to the future, think comprehensively and collectively, and build upon and surpass your initial vision. Translate complexity into a clear, positive and ambitious mission, composed of possible steps and available resources: make what is complicated easy and simple, in order to encourage people to join your cause.
- Engage the **motivation** of your employees. Publicise tasks, encourage initiative and give constructive feedback, whatever the result. Celebrate success and have fun, even in meetings: you will strengthen the feeling of

belonging and pride in the group.

- Be an **example** to those around you: do what you say and keep your promises; participate in team tasks and complete challenges; stay up to date and continue to develop your talents. You will gain confidence and credibility.
- Seek **performance**, freeing up your time and resources that you can use to continue to progress.
- Do not be afraid of **change**: anticipate it. Take time to reflect and seek advice from your surroundings, and let people convince you if their argument is valid. Experiment to innovate and find better ways to achieve your goals. Change your procedures. Evolve, whilst staying true to yourself.
- Take **risks**. Nobody achieves greatness without failures. Leaders are recognised by their ability to bounce back; accept your mistakes and learn from them.
- Develop your strength of **conviction**. Learn how to make your case at any time. Show your talents as a speaker by encouraging, persuading, negotiating, promoting and defending your ideas and your team. Of course, adapt your approach to your audience. Put some heart and enthusiasm into your words.
- Remember that **communicating** is all about listening to the other person and their needs. Make sure you understand their point of view by reformulating it.

FAQS

WHAT ARE THE 12 ESSENTIAL QUALITIES OF A GOOD LEADER?

- Integrity
- Enthusiasm
- Charisma
- Setting a good example
- Good memory
- Communication
- Vision
- Judgment
- Decisiveness
- Ability to delegate
- Ability to lighten the mood
- Ability to identify resources and mobilise them efficiently and effectively.

CAN A MANAGER BECOME A LEADER?

There are some managers who do not provide leadership, but still do their job very well. They do not necessarily need leadership skills. They are able to manage the teams and activities under their responsibility remarkably well, without bringing innovative ideas, influencing or inspiring their employees, as they leave this task to their superiors. There are companies that are happy to employ operational managers who are not seeking to exercise leadership.

Of course, a manager can evolve into a leader by taking the

time to think about the emotional side of managing a team and using their ability to generate commitment and enthusiasm from employees. Leadership is learned and everyone, if they desire, can develop their leadership skills.

CAN A LEADER BECOME A MANAGER?

Yes, but beware that there are some incompetent leaders in management. They may not have a sense of operationality, concreteness or the organisation of work. A leader can therefore excel in their influence and inspiration, perhaps providing the company with new perspectives, but may not be competent at structuring the work.

Being a manager and possessing leadership skills go hand in hand, sometimes being divided between several people and other times being merged into one.

HOW CAN I GAIN THE TRUST OF MY TEAM?

It is impossible to lead a team towards a goal without gaining their confidence. Here are five dimensions of trust that you should aim for (Schindler and Thomas, 1993).

- Integrity: consistency between the words and actions of the leader.
- Competence: skills, knowledge and the ability to delegate.
- Consistency: consistency between the actions and discernment of the leader.
- Loyalty: loyalty to objectives, with no opportunism from the leader.

- Openness: possibility for everyone to express themselves without repercussions.

> "Blue Antidote is a start-up that aims to equip commercial delegates from pharmaceutical companies through the use of iPad applications. These applications allow sales teams to better communicate the value of the health products they offer.
>
> As the founder of the project, I surround myself with experts with pointed and complementary profiles to create and launch a prototype. I am mainly interested in individual skills, whether pharmaceutical or in the field of software development. The team is centred around an innovative project.
>
> At first, our meetings were very intense exchanges with many explanations. Everyone needed to understand the mission. My role was to manage the orientation of each member. For the project, it was crucial to build confidence within the team, with customers and with partners. We had to prove that the idea could work.
>
> The start-up has grown according to feedback and is constantly improving. As the start-up grows, each member of the team becomes more autonomous. We can continue to develop new projects." – *Augustin Terlinden – Founder, Blue Antidote*

HOW CAN I RESTORE MY LEADERSHIP IF POWER GAMES HAVE DISRUPTED MY TEAM?

As the head of a team full of strong personalities, you may find yourself in trouble. Identify what you need to reposition yourself: training, coaching, hierarchical support? It is clear that you will need to establish your identity in order to strengthen your leadership.

To restore a more equal relationship, do not hesitate to speak to your manager. Directors must help their management team in a leadership dispute and you should not have the slightest doubt that your management will support team leaders. This is fundamental. The employee, even if using their own leadership skills, must understand that their manager remains the leader.

Help them in their work, but pay no attention to their influence games. You can also invite them to apply for a position with more responsibilities. Assertiveness will help here. Do not cut the growing wings of a future collaborator. Help them to develop a constructive or businesslike attitude. Allow ideas to appear through collective intelligence: "Shared leadership can be the most effective!" (Gibeault, 2012).

IS IT MANIPULATIVE TO EXERCISE LEADERSHIP?

Leadership is not manipulation. A manipulator aims to meet their own objectives by exerting influence without respect for the freedom of thought of others. Leadership, however, is the ability to influence others to agree to mobilise on behalf of a cause, a purpose, or because they want to.

People give leaders legitimate recognition. By asserting themselves, leaders do not hesitate to express their wishes with conviction, but without aggression. A leader listens and accepts that there are opinions that differ from their own. They seek to manage conflict and may exercise their bargaining power to find a win-win solution.

WHAT SHOULD A LEADER DO IN AN ORGANISATION WHERE LEADERSHIP IS NOT VALUED?

Start by taking a step back and asking the right questions: do you accept your mission and the values of your company? Do you participate mindfully? Is your leadership style what the organisation expects of you? Is there mutual trust? Do you lack experience?

Work to develop your professional and personal skills as much as possible, and if no door is open to you and you cannot find fulfilment in your work, it is certainly better to find a company that better matches your personality. Why not even create your own job?

OVER TO YOU

Here is a six-step method and tips to develop your career in business and move from being a manager to becoming a leader (Ram Charan and Stephen Drotter, 2010).

1. You cannot become a manager without first knowing how to manage yourself. This begins by taking a step back to observe and improve professional and personal skills. Identify your piloting projects, but avoid only sticking to an operational approach. Ask yourself the following questions often: "Why am I doing this?", "Am I doing this correctly?" and "How can I do this better?".

   ### ACTIVITY

   Introduce yourself to management by transitioning from an effective collaborator to a manager. You will learn to share responsibilities with each member of your project team.

2. The second step is to manage others by giving them goals and means. Learn to evaluate your team, give feedback and encourage them to do better.

   ### ACTIVITY

   Evaluate challenges and resources. Manage power games (group influence and coalitions).

3. You will take a big step forward if you learn to manage the managers. You then step away from an operational role, to a functional role. You will learn to give more challenging goals and manage the relationships between team leaders. Your leadership will be tested.

ACTIVITY

Strengthen your social relationships, direct yourself more towards financial management and reporting.

4. Become a good functional manager by taking responsibility for a service. Consolidate your people and budget management skills by excelling in data management strategies.

ACTIVITY

Understand your environment completely. Establish a vision. Bring your team to the next level by developing the talents of your employees. Find additional resources and efficient procedures. Turn your team into a dream team that is proactive and ready to follow you. Everything relies on the mutual trust that you have co-constructed.

5. Next, you are the manager of a division. You demonstrate your ability to manage several organisations at the same time. You become an even more important strategic player.

Stay true to yourself, your vision and your values. Take a step back to maintain your social relationships, both professional and personal, to manage stress and to nourish your vision. Pay attention to major issues and ethical questions.

6. Finally, the director. Based on trust, your leadership gives your management team the task of running your organisation. All you need to do is provide the broad guidelines, based on your vision and values that are known by the team.

ACTIVITY

Maintain clear and accurate communication of your principles, stay optimistic and spend time and energy encouraging your employees to make the necessary changes. Pay close attention to your environment and, if necessary, be prepared to change everything by building a support network that is ready to mobilise to your vision.

A career is built with experience. Becoming a top leader can be achieved by stepping outside of your comfort zone to try new challenges, each with increasing responsibilities.

We want to hear from you!
Leave a comment on your online library
and share your favourite books on social media!

FURTHER READING

BIBLIOGRAPHY

- Bar-On, R. (2006) The Bar-On model of emotional-social intelligence (ESI). *Psicotema.* Vol 18, pp.13-25.
- Blake, R. and Mouton, J. (1987) *La troisième dimension du management.* Paris: Éditions d'Organisation.
- Charan, R., Drotter, S. and Noel, J. (2011) *The Leadership Pipeline: How to Build the Leadership Powered Company.* San Francisco: Jossey-Bass.
- Getz, I. and Carney, B.M. (2012) *Liberté & Cie : Quand la liberté des salariés fait le bonheur des entreprises.* Paris: Fayard.
- Gibeault, D. (2012) Forum Ouvert – Incitation au leadership partagé et à la responsabilisation. *Livre Black sur le Forum Ouvert.* C. Koehler, ed. Paris: Forum Ouvert. pp.13-17.
- Hersey, P. and Blanchard, K. H. (1977) *Management of Organizational Behavior: Utilizing Human Resources.* Englewood Cliffs (NJ): Prentice Hall.
- Kets de Vries, M.F.R. (2008) Arcétypes de leadership et équipe de direction. *Gestion.* Vol. 33, pp. 48-60.
- Kotter, J.P. (1999) Qu'est- ce que le leadership? *Harvard Business Review. Le leadership.* Paris: Éditions d'Organisation, pp. 40-61.
- Kouzes, J.M. and Posner, B. (2012) *The Leadership Challenge: How to make extraordinary things happen in organizations.* 5th edition. San Francisco: Jossey-Bass.
- Human Resource Department (2009) *Les principles de gestion et de "leadership" chez Nestlé.* Vevey (Suisse):

Nestlé. [Online]. [Accessed 3 August 2016]. Available from: <http://www.nestle.ch/asset-library/documents/jobs/managementleadershp_fr.pdf>

- Schindler, P.L. and Thomas, C.C. (1993) The structure of interpersonal trust in the workplace. *Psychological Reports*. 73(2), pp. 563-573.
- Zaleznik, A. (1999) Managers et leaders, en quoi sont-ils différents? *Harvard Business Review. Le leadership*. Paris: Éditions d'Organisation, pp. 62-87.

ADDITIONAL SOURCES

- Cherret de la Boissiere, A. (2009) *Leadership au masculin et au féminin. Le management aux valeurs mixtes : l'avenir de l'entreprise*. Paris: Dunod.
- Deering, A. and Robert, D. (2009) *Alpha Leadership. Les 3 A: Anticiper, Aligner, Agir*. Louvain-la-Neuve/Paris: De Boeck.
- Duluc, A. (2013) *Leadership et confiance. Jouer collectif, parler vrai, être humain*. 3rd edition. Paris: Dunod.
- Kotsou, I. (2012) *Intelligence émotionnelle et management : Comprendre et utiliser la force des émotions*. Louvain-la-Neuve/Paris: De Boeck.
- Maxwell, J.C. (2003) *Leadership, 101 principes de base. Ce que tout leader devrait savoir*. Québec: Un monde différent.
- Robert, D. (2009) *Leadership visionnaire. Outils et compétences pour réussir le changement par la PNL*. Louvain-la-Neuve/Paris: De Boeck.
- Testa, J.P. Lafargue, J. and Tilhet-Coartet, V. (2013) *La Boîte à outils du Leadership*. Paris: Dunod.